George Washington
CROSSWORD PUZZLES

USA GRAB A PENCIL PRESS

CARLISLE, MASSACHUSETTS

George Washington Crossword Puzzles

Copyright © 2014 Applewood Books, Inc.

ISBN : 978-0-9836416-0-5

Published by
GRAB A PENCIL PRESS
an imprint of Applewood Books
Carlisle, Massachusetts 01741
www.grabapencilpress.com

10 9 8 7 6 5 4 3 2

Manufactured in the United States of America

George Washington
CROSSWORD PUZZLES

Known as the "Father of Our Country," George Washington was instrumental in forming America's government. Born in Virginia in 1732, Washington never received a formal education but was instead taught by his half-brothers. As a teenager, he began working as a surveyor before entering the military.

After fighting in the French and Indian War, Washington led Continental forces during the American Revolution and became a national hero. He presided over the Constitutional Convention and was unanimously elected to be the first president of the new United States.

As president, Washington surrounded himself with other forefathers — Thomas Jefferson, Alexander Hamilton, John Adams, and John Jay were all members of his cabinet. Soon, conflict rose between Hamilton and Jefferson, and Washington found himself in the middle. Never wanting to involve America in another war, Washington remained neutral in foreign affairs. Washington worked hard to abide by the Constitution and to help the country through the aftermath of the Revolution. The Whiskey Rebellion of 1792 tested his presidency, but Washington was able to peacefully end the conflict. It is largely through his patriotism and dedication that America thrived as a nation.

After leaving office, Washington was called to serve again as commander of the Army. He also was involved in the planning and designing of the national city, which would become Washington, D.C. He retired to his beloved plantation, Mount Vernon, which he renovated and built up to be a beautiful testament to architecture, as well as a personal haven.

George Washington died in December 1799, never living to see the completion of the national city. His birthday, February 22nd, is celebrated throughout the country as Presidents Day. His spirit lives on in the many national landmarks that bear his name.

PUZZLE ANSWERS ON BACK PAGES

Before He Was President

ACROSS

2. Born in Westmoreland County, Virginia on the 22nd of this month in 1732

4. After England imposed the Townshend Acts, Washington and George _____ called for a boycott of British goods

6. Washington's half-brothers were sent to this country to receive their formal education

9. Believing education to be very important, he left money in his will to set up a school in this northern Virginia city

10. Washington's favorite school subject

12. Washington wanted to join the British _____ when he was a teenager, but his mother refused to consent

14. Chosen as a representative to the _____ Congress in 1774

15. First name of Washington's wife, who was a widow with two children when they married

18. Traveled to this British island colony with his half-brother Lawrence

19. Inherited the family plantation, Mount _____, in 1752

20. Expanded his plantation from two thousand to _____ thousand acres

DOWN

1. George Washington did not go to _____. He stopped going to school when he was 15

3. Name of Washington's father, who served as a justice on the county court

5. Moved to a plantation in this Virginia city in 1738, where he spent much of his youth

7. Name of Washington's mother

8. One fable about Washington is that he threw a silver dollar across this river

11. Contracted this disease in his late teens

13. Became a _____ while still a teen, measuring and charting the land of the new country

16. Elected to the _____ of Burgesses in 1758

17. Replacing tobacco, this became Washington's major cash crop in the 1760s

Washington the Warrior —
The French and Indian War

ACROSS

1. Washington first entered the military by joining this colony's militia

3. During one battle in the French and Indian War, Washington had two

_____

shot out from under him

7. In 1758, the British finally gained control of the

_____

River Valley, a strategic location of the war

8. Robert Dinwiddie,

_____ of Virginia, sent Washington on a 900-mile journey to deliver a message to the French demanding they retreat

9. The Treaty of _____ of 1763 ended the war and France gave up its claims on Canada

10. Washington met with Legardeur de St. Pierre, the

highest _____ official, to order him and his troops to leave

13. Washington resigned his commission, but in 1755 returned to serve as a _____ aide to General Edward Braddock

14. Washington's guide in the early stages of the French and Indian War suffered _____ due to extreme cold near the Allegheny River

16. The first French settlement in North America was _____, in Canada in 1603, while England settled Jamestown in 1607

17. Washington _____ the first battle of the French and Indian War

DOWN

2. "Half-King" was the chief of this Indian tribe

4. The French and Indian War is referred to as the _____ Years War in Canada

5. Washington's account of his expeditions was published in both Williamsburg, Virginia and this English city

6. In 1775, Washington was commissioned by _____ to lead the Continental Army, a position that kept him away from home for eight years

11. In 1753, French troops started moving south from Canada to build forts near this Great Lake

12. In the late 1750s, Washington was given _____ of Virginia's entire military force

15. Several Indian tribes fought alongside Washington because of a _____ between them and the British

The Road to Revolution

ACROSS

3. Britain's monarch during the Revolutionary War was King _____ III

6. In 1780, General Charles _____ became commander of British forces

7. Washington led the _____ Army during the American Revolution

9. Under the Treaty of Paris, Canada remained under British control while Florida was returned to this country

10. In 1778, the British began targeting sites in the South, capturing Charleston, South Carolina, and this Georgia city

11. During the 1760s and 1770s, England imposed many _____ on American colonists, including the Stamp Act, the Townshend Acts, and the Coercive Acts, which led to colonial protests, as Americans had no representatives in British Parliament

13. Low on food and supplies, Washington's army spent a hard winter at Valley _____

14. In April 1775, fighting between the British and colonists erupted at Lexington and Concord, in what is now this state

15. After heavy defeats throughout New York, Washington crossed the _____ River and won several battles in New Jersey

16. Thousands of _____ Americans fought on the British side in hopes of gaining their freedom

17. Some _____ Americans supported Great Britain in order to protect their land from colonists, though others supported the American cause

DOWN

1. Not only a war between nations, the American Revolution was also a _____ war, as some colonists remained loyal to the king and fought alongside the British

2. After a colonial victory at Saratoga, New York, this European country became our ally, lending its military and naval forces to the colonists

4. On July 4th, 1776, the colonies declared their _____ from Britain

5. Though Britain repealed many taxes, it did not repeal the tax on tea, thus leading to the Boston Tea _____, a colonial uprising that destroyed British goods and contributed to the Revolution

8. In September 1783, the war ended with the signing of the Treaty of Paris, which made the _____ River America's western border

12. The siege of _____ resulted in a pivotal America victory and British surrender

13. Benjamin _____, John Jay, and John Adams represented the colonies during peace negotiations

The U.S. Constitution

ACROSS

4. Though only 27 have been approved, more than 11,000 _____ to the Constitution have been proposed

8. There are this many branches of government

9. The Bill of _____, which guarantees freedom of press, assembly, religion, speech, and other freedoms, was added to the Constitution later

10. This state was the first to ratify the Constitution

11. George Washington called the Constitution "little short of a _____"

13. George Washington was appointed commander of the _____ Army in the same building where the Constitution was later signed

16. Thomas Jefferson was in this country when the Constitution was signed

17. The House of Representatives and the Senate make up the two houses of Congress. Each state has two senators, while the number of representatives for a state depends on _____

DOWN

1. The 17th of this month is celebrated as the anniversary of the signing of the Constitution

2. Those who opposed the Constitution were called anti-_____

3. The Supreme Court is part of this branch of government

4. The Constitution can be viewed at the National _____ in Washington, D.C.

5. Rhode Island and North Carolina didn't ratify the Constitution until Washington was inaugurated as _____

6. Under the Constitution, the president has the power to nominate and appoint ambassadors, ministers, and Supreme Court judges, with Senate approval. The President also serves as the _____ in chief of the country's armed forces

7. The majority of the population of this state was against ratifying the Constitution (two words)

12. James _____ was the first delegate to arrive at the Constitutional Convention

14. The Constitution needed to be approved by this many states to go into effect

15. George Washington, who was elected to preside over the Constitutional Convention, worked very hard to get states to _____ it

The First President of the United States

WHITE HOUSE HISTORICAL ASSOCIATION

ACROSS

3. Washington devoted much of his first term to shaping the new _____ government

10. The original _____ Court consisted of five associate justices and one chief justice

11. Washington took over treaty negotiations with the _____ Nation of Native Americans to avoid further domestic war

12. The British wanted _____ Americans to attack American settlers in the West in an effort to weaken the new nation

13. This northern city was the site of Washington's first inauguration

14. Washington sent General "Mad" Anthony Wade to crush a coalition of seven Indian _____, all of whom were forced to move west following defeat

15. Washington is the only president to have been _____ elected

17. John _____ received the second-most number of votes, making him vice president

18. In 1789, this European country, who aided the Americans during their struggle for independence, began their own revolution

DOWN

1. Post-war America had mounting national and foreign _____. How to pay these off was a topic of hot debate

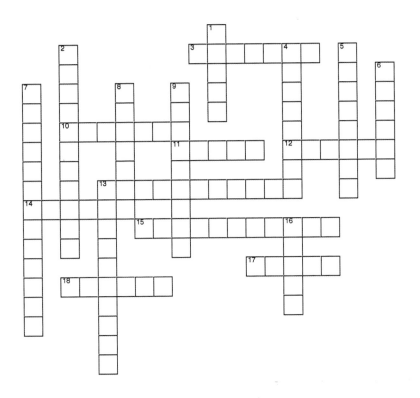

2. Washington believed the executive branch could act without the approval of Congress, part of this branch, during foreign conflicts

4. The Departments of War, State, and Treasury, as well as the office of _____ General were established during Washington's presidency

5. With Washington's signing of the Judiciary Act of 1789, this branch was created

6. The 1794 Battle of _____ Timbers, fought between American forces and Native Americans, resulted in several hundred Native American deaths

7. He was planning on retiring after the _____ War, but Americans called on Washington to be their president

8. Disputes between cabinet members led to the formation of political _____, something Washington had wanted to avoid

9. The _____ College chose Washington as president in 1788

13. Washington made a Declaration of _____ in hopes of avoiding involvement in foreign conflicts

16. Though Washington wanted to expand westward, he was halted by territorial issues with this country until the last years of his presidency

Washington's Men

ACROSS

5. Thomas Jefferson once wrote in a letter to James _____- that "a little rebellion now and then is a good thing"

8. John Adams called the vice presidency "the most _____ office"

9. Alexander Hamilton served as George Washington's Secretary of _____

10. Jefferson served as Washington's Secretary of _____

CITY OF PHILADELPHIA

DOWN

1. James Madison and Thomas Jefferson founded the _____-Republic Party

2. First name of Adams' wife, who was influential in his politics

3. Madison helped establish freedom of _____ while at the 1776 Virginia Convention. This freedom was later included in the Bill of Rights

4. Hamilton, Madison, and John Jay wrote the Federalist Papers in support of the ratification of the U.S. _____

WHITE HOUSE HISTORICAL ASSOCIATION

13. Adams lost re-election to Thomas Jefferson in 1800. Both men died on the _____ of July, 1826

15. Madison supported the abolition of _____

16. Alexander Hamilton and Thomas _____ argued over the economy and foreign policy, leading to the creation of political parties

WHITE HOUSE

6. Alexander Hamilton was born on the British island of Nevis to unmarried parents. He was sent to this colony to be educated and later joined the American militia

7. John Adams and Thomas Jefferson were appointed to the committee that drafted the Declaration of _____

11. Henry Knox was a general in the Continental _____ during the American Revolution and became friends with Washington while serving under him

12. Jefferson believed in the separation of _____ and state. He founded the University of Virginia, the first American university not centered around religion

14. Washington's Secretary of _____ was Henry Knox

Washington's Second Term

ACROSS

3. _____ Jay was sent to Great Britain to negotiate a treaty, known as the Jay Treaty, which was greatly debated by Congress but approved by Washington

4. To stop the Whiskey Rebellion, Washington sent _____ to control the resistance and later went there himself

7. Great Britain tried to stop _____ between the United States and the French Caribbean and West Indian ports

8. Of the French Revolution, Thomas Jefferson stated that it was "only to be expected that the _____ of liberty must sometimes be watered by human blood"

12. _____ XVI, King of France, was executed by the opposition, leading to the French Revolution

14. Citizens of this state attacked money collectors and formed resistance movements, leading to the Whiskey Rebellion

15. The _____ narrowly approved the Jay Treaty, which imposed severe trade restrictions on the U.S., leading to widespread debate and further division of political parties

16. Newspapers of this political party began to publicly criticize Washington after the Jay Treaty controversy

U. S. SENATE

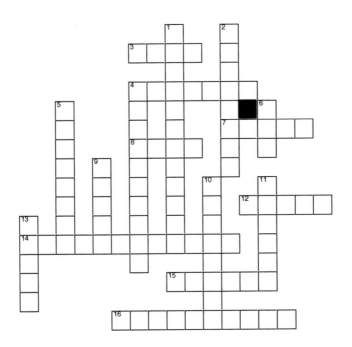

DOWN

1. Washington's second inauguration took place in this Pennsylvania city

2. Citizen Edmond Genet was France's _____ to America. He worked to gain American support of France's revolution, but was met with criticism by Washington

4. Thomas Jefferson resigned as secretary of state in 1793 to retire to his Virginia home of _____. He was replaced by Edmund Randolph

5. Due to France's aid during the _____ Revolution, the United States promised to help France in the event of war. However, Washington wanted to avoid involvement in the international conflict and remained neutral

6. A _____ on whiskey was imposed during the 1790s

9. Following Washington's retirement, John _____ was elected as the second president of the United States

10. Washington supported a _____ bank, heralded by Hamilton. This caused a rift between the president and Jefferson, as well as others

11. James _____ served as U.S. minister to France until 1796, when Washington replaced him with Charles Pinckney

13. A treaty with this country opened up the Mississippi River to the United States and made it the country's western border

Mount Vernon

ACROSS

4. Mount Vernon sits on the _____ River

6. The building's cupola allowed cool drafts to be ventilated through the house and out open _____

12. Washington commissioned William Sears, an indentured _____ working for George Mason, to carve a chimney piece for Mount Vernon's small dining room

13. Washington's _____ built the original house, and his half-brother Lawrence rebuilt it in the 1740s

14. Washington's Mount Vernon is an impressive example of _____ era architecture

15. During Washington's first remodeling of Mount Vernon, he was fighting in the French and _____ War

16. An arcade, a series of _____, is an architectural feature of Mount Vernon

DOWN

1. Washington has been compared to Cincinnatus, the brief _____ emperor who left after serving his country to return to farming

2. Lund Washington, a cousin of George, managed the plantation while Washington was leading the _____ Army during the Revolutionary War

MOUNT VERNON

3. Of farming, Washington commented, "When I speak of a knowing farmer, I mean one who understands the best course of crops; how to plow and sow, to mow, to hedge, to Ditch and above all, Midas like, one who can convert everything he touches into manure, as the first transmutation towards _____."

5. Mount Vernon's _____-story portico is the most copied feature in American architecture

7. Washington designed a barn with _____ sides to make it appear round, and therefore easy for animals to tread

8. Of the remodeling, Washington stated, "I shall begrudge no reasonable expense that will contribute to the improvement and neatness of my farms, for nothing pleases me _____ than to see them in good order ... nor nothing hurts me more than to find them otherwise."

9. A pediment, _____ in shape, was added in 1774, as well as a piazza and cupola

10. Washington employed many of his _____ to help during renovations by training them in carpentry, painting, blacksmithing, and other trades

11. Mount Vernon's piazza, paved with flagstone, was designed to unite outdoor and _____ spaces

12. The Main Mansion has three floors and is roughly _____ thousand square feet

13. An exterior wall is known as a _____

Washington's Dream of Washington, D.C.

ACROSS

3. The _____ Act gave Washington the power to choose the site for the capital city, as well as three commissioners to carry out plans

4. Pierre L'Enfant, from this country, served as city planner until he was replaced by Andrew and Benjamin Ellicott

8. While eccentric L'Enfant planned the city, Washington remained at _____ _____, his family residence near Alexandria. While there, Washington worried about L'Enfant's grandiose and massive plans

10. The Capitol building and the president's house were destroyed during the _____ of 1812

12. Though instrumental in its planning, George Washington died six months before Washington officially became the seat of federal _____

13. President Washington had to obtain title _____ from landowners in order to build the city, a very difficult task

16. Washington explored many sites before choosing to build the national city in Virginia and this state

17. After being fired, L'Enfant refused a lot next to the president's house. In 1825, he died in poverty and was later buried at _____ National Cemetery

18. Circular intersections were built to revolve around the _____ House and the Capitol building

L ENFANT

ARCHITECT OF THE CAPITOL

DOWN

1. Meeting at a tavern in this part of D.C., Washington convinced landowners to sell their land for $66 an acre

2. Originally, Washington called D.C. "_____ City," combining the terms "Federal Town" and "Capital City"

5. Washington D.C.'s streets were given simple names based on numbers and _____

6. Philadelphia temporarily served as the nation's capital.; the Continental _____ convened there

7. This avenue connects the White House with the Capitol building

9. The largest avenue Pierre L'Enfant designed for D.C. was 400 feet wide and one mile long. It is now occupied by the _____ Mall

11. Washington, D.C. is built along this river

14. There was much debate over whether to build the capital in the North or in the South. Because of this, two national cities were almost built, the other to be built along this river

15. This president was the first to reside in Washington, D.C.

In Washington's Words

ACROSS

2. There is but one _____ course, and that is to seek truth and pursue it steadily

5. "Human happiness and _____ duty are inseparably connected."

7. "It is better to offer no excuse than a _____ one"

8. "Gentlemen, you will permit me to put on my spectacles, for, I have grown not only gray, but almost _____ in the service of my country"

10. "It is better to be _____ than in bad company"

13. "By the all-powerful dispensations of Providence, I have been protected beyond all human probability and expectation; for I had four _____ through my coat, and two horses shot under me, yet escaped unhurt, altho' death was levelling my companions on every side"

14. In an address to the Continental Army, Washington stated, "The fate of unborn millions will now depend, under God, on the courage and conduct of this army. Our cruel and unrelenting enemy leaves us only the choice of brave resistance, or the most abject submission. We have therefore to resolve to conquer or to _____."

15. "The harder the conflict, the _____ the triumph."

16. Upon being elected president, Washington said "I feel very much like a man who is condemned to _____ does when the time of his execution draws nigh."

DOWN

1. "Labor to keep alive in your chest that little spark of celestial _____ called conscience".

2. "If freedom of _____ is taken away, then dumb and silent we may be led, like sheep to the slaughter"

3. "A bad war is fought with a _____ mind"

4. "Be courteous to _____, but intimate with few, and let those few be well tried before you give them your confidence"

5. "I have always considered _____ as the most interesting event of one's life, the foundation of happiness or misery."

6. "I can only say that there is not a man living who wishes more sincerely than I do to see a plan adopted for the _____ of it (slavery)"

9. "I hope I shall always possess firmness and virtue enough to maintain what I consider the most enviable of all titles, the character of an _____ man"

11. I beg it may be remembered by every gentleman in the room, that I this day declare with the utmost sincerity I do not think myself _____ to the command I am honored with."

12. I leave you with undefiled hands — an uncorrupted heart — and with ardent vows to heaven for the welfare & happiness of that country in which I and my forefathers drew our first _____

George Washington Trivia

ACROSS

4. Washington is the only president that did not live in the _____ House

5. Washington is the only president to free all of his _____. His estate even paid for their care after his death

9. A vault was built under the U.S. _____ building that was intended to hold the remains of George Washington after his death. However, he was buried at Mount Vernon

11. Upon hearing of Washington's intention to retire as Commander of the Continental Forces, King George III said, "If he does that, he will be the greatest man in the _____"

12. Washington did not wear a _____, but he did powder his hair

14. Washington's favorite food was this cold dessert

16. Though regarded as the "Father of Our _____," he fathered no children of his own

17. Washington proposed to Martha after only knowing her for _____ weeks

DOWN

1. George Washington's great-granddaughter married Robert E. _____, leader of the Confederate Army during the Civil War

2. This holiday was first celebrated during Washington's presidency

3. During Washington's presidency, five states were added to the Union: Rhode Island, Kentucky, Vermont, Tennessee, and North _____

6. Washington is credited with bringing the mule to the United States by mating horses with donkeys. The first donkey he received was from the king of this country

7. Washington was the only U.S. president to die during this century

8. When greeting visitors, George Washington would _____ to them. Thomas Jefferson later changed this custom, instead shaking hands with visitors

10. Washington bred hound dogs. Two of them were named Sweet Lips and True _____

13. Washington owned six white horses and he ordered that their _____ be brushed every morning

15. By the time Washington became president, he had this many teeth left, and had to use false teeth

16. A popular myth about George Washington is that, as a young boy, he chopped down this type of tree

ARCHITECT OF THE CAPITOL

Where's Washington?

ACROSS

1. Washington's face, along with those of Thomas Jefferson, Abraham Lincoln, and Theodore Roosevelt, is carved on Mount _____

5. Washington's birthday is now nationally celebrated as _____ Day

7. The Apotheosis of George Washington, an intricate and ornate painting by Constantino Brumidi in 1865 , can be seen in the U.S. _____ building

8. The USS George Washington is a U.S. _____ ship

10. Our nation's capital, Washington D.C., was named after George Washington. "D.C." stands for "District of _____"

13. Washington state was named after our first president. A city there is named this

15. A Freemason, a National _____ Memorial is dedicated to him

16. Washington's profile can be seen on this U.S. coin

DOWN

2. Established in 1821, George Washington _____ fulfilled Washington's vision of an institution in the nation's capital dedicated to educating future leaders

3. The 555-foot tall Washington National _____ stands in Washington, D.C.

4. The George Washington Memorial Parkway runs along the _____ River

6. Artist Jonathan Trumbull created many works depicting the _____ War, one of which shows General Cornwallis surrendering to Washington

8. The George Washington Bridge connects New York to this state

9. A statue of Washington stands in Trafalgar Square in this English city

SEE CLUE 1 ACROSS

11. Washington's image is on the _____ dollar bill

12. In 1840, Horatio Greenough created a statue of Washington based on a famous statue of this Greek god. It now sits in the National Museum of American History

14. Washington's face was on one of the United States' first _____ stamps. His image has been used on more stamps than any other American

PUZZLE ANSWERS

Before He Was President

Washington the Warrior

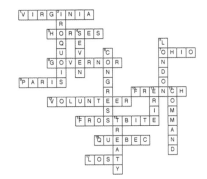

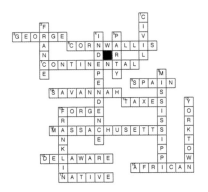

The Road to Revolution

The U.S. Constitution

The First President of the United States

Washington's Men

Washington's Second Term

Washington's Mount Vernon

Washington's Dream of Washington, D.C.

RESIDENCE · FRANCE · MOUNT VERNON · WAR · GOVERNMENT · DEEDS · MARYLAND · ARLINGTON · WHITE

In Washington's Words

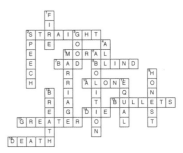

STRAIGHT · MORAL · BAD · BLIND · ALONE · BULLETS · DIE · GREATER · DEATH

George Washington Trivia

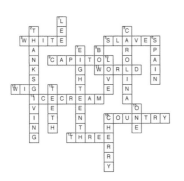

WHITE · SLAVES · CAPITOL · WORLD · WIG · ICECREAM · COUNTRY · THREE

Where's Washington?

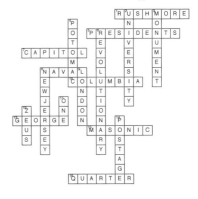

RUSHMORE · PRESIDENTS · CAPITOL · NAVAL · COLUMBIA · GEORGE · MASONIC · QUARTER

GRAB A PENCIL PRESS

Abraham Lincoln

American Flag

American Revolution

Architecture

Art History

Benjamin Franklin

Black History

Civil War History

Ellis Island and the Statue of Liberty

First Ladies

George Washington

Gold Rush

John Fitzgerald Kennedy

Korean War

National Parks

Natural History

New York City

Presidents of the United States

Secret Writing

Texas History

Thanksgiving

Vietnam War

Washington, D.C.

Women's History

World War II

World War II European Theater

World War II Pacific Theater

Yellowstone National Park

COMING SOON

Flight Puzzle Book

Library of Congress Puzzle Book

World War I Puzzle Book

USA GRAB A PENCIL PRESS

an imprint of Applewood Books
Carlisle, Massachusetts 01741
www.grabapencilpress.com

To order, call: 800-277-5312